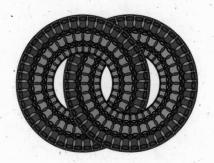

PLACES

I WAS

DREAMING

PLACES

I WAS

DREAMING

LOREN GRAHAM

CavanKerry ◈ Press LTD.

CavanKerry Press Ltd.
Fort Lee, New Jersey
www.cavankerrypress.org

Publisher's Cataloging-in-Publication
(Provided by Quality Books, Inc.)

Graham, Loren, 1958-
[Poems. Selections]
Places I was dreaming / Loren Graham. -- First
edition.
pages cm
Poems.
ISBN 978-1-933880-45-7

I. Title.

PS3557.R2154P53 2015   811'.54
QBI14-600182

Cover photograph by NatuerlichGut, Pixabay
Cover and interior text design by Gregory Smith
First Edition 2015, Printed in the United States of America

CavanKerry Press is dedicated to springboarding the careers of previously unpublished, early, and mid-career poets by bringing to print two to three Emerging Voices annually. Manuscripts are selected from open submission; Cavankerry Press does not conduct competitions.

CavanKerry Press is grateful for the support it receives from the New Jersey State Council on the Arts.

Also by Loren Graham

Mose (1994)

The Ring Scar (2010)

CONTENTS

AN OCCURRENCE ON THE BLUEBIRD

THE TIME I DIDN'T DROWN

PLACES

I WAS

DREAMING

THE HOUSE

The House

Kids on the school bus claimed it was haunted,
claimed no one lived there, said "no one could,"
dared themselves to go there, got no takers

for the two-story wreck set back from the road
(dirt road close by the new subdivision)
backed by acres of broom grass and scrub,

crookedy tower that never saw paint,
house forever gray and falling
whose roof shed fragments continually,

green crumbles of asphalt that rained on the yard,
on the coal stove that summered on the rotting porch,
on the hulks of eviscerated cars that attended.

House with ramshackle outhouse behind,
with well, with chicken house covered in tin,
rusting stock tank, tumbledown barns.

House of clapboard warped and gapping,
house with bees inside its walls,
house rats frequented.

Pile of loosening plaster and lath,
eyesore clucked at and pitied,
object of dread and erosion:

Yes. Yes. That house.
The one I called *my house,*
our house, home.

THE FIRST
THING I
REMEMBER

The First Thing I Remember

When this hand was three   *when this hand was much smaller*
they came forth to claim it   *their little claws on it*
to smell it, to tongue it   *to fondle with incisors*
in the long old darkness   *my unknowing sleep*

When this arm could not harm them   *when this arm was tender*
the killers of chickens   *the gnawers through floors*
walked over its sinews   *traversed its small muscles*
dragging their tails   *like skinny dead worms*

When these ribs were new   *while this chest breathed easy*
a ghostly thing sat here   *a yellow-toothed guest*
used this for its lookout   *rested here on hind feet*
its forepaws held high   *as it sniffed the night*

When these legs were short   *when this body was no cipher*
the destroyers of grain   *they crept over me freely*
paused to scratch fleas   *stopped there to give gifts*
pissed and left droppings   *on white sheets in the dark*

And what ever stopped it   *that midnight possession*
A chiseled tooth cut me   *gouged deep between fingers*
and I cried out I howled   *the way we all have to*
when the long darkness rises   *when it sniffs at our ears*

I did what is in us   *cried out and was heard*
and the lights came on bright   *and it opened before me*
the first thing I remember   *this hand in blood*
those brown shadows fleeing   *those naked tails*

Small Child Walking on Great Aunts and Uncles

They lined up like foothills on our flowered divan,
the great ones, overflowing the kitchen chairs and footstools
that continued in a circle across the front room linoleum,
and I climbed up to travel the uneven track of their laps.

I trod on the scruffy ones, the gap-toothed, the jowly.
The oblong of bosom who smelled of talcum and coffee.
Those who laughed themselves red in the face.
I walked across the paunchy and the ones with unruly hair.
The warty. The blemished. The slope-shouldered and dewlapped.
Those whose breath came out in little gasps.

I traversed shaky lipstick and eyebrows drawn on in pencil,
the bald, bespectacled, chinless,
those with an air of motor oil and fish bait,
with huge meaty hands and over-inflated fingers,
those who scraped under their nails with knife blades.
The ones who laughed hard in odd wheezes and grunts.
The ones who laughed merely by shaking.

Mine was a road of scratchers and nodders,
a pathway of great jiggling elbows,
of the stubby, of the widow's-peaked, of gaping black nostrils,
a fleshy track suffused with tobacco and bacon grease.
These were the ground I walked on, mine underfoot,
and though dead are still mine and will persist as mine
though I be trod with them, though I be dust.

Fate

It is easy to see that I wouldn't have fallen
into the remnants of a scrapwood fire
at the age of four, shirtless fortunately,

and burned my whole arm, wrist to shoulder,
if Mom hadn't been cooking in the yard that week,
on half a rusty metal oil drum

that she wrestled into place nightly over the fire—
which she wouldn't have *had* to do if we had had any propane
for the kitchen cookstove—which we *would* have had

if the money had been there from the sale of the hogs
that we *would* have had that summer, if the sickness
that made them all worthless hadn't gotten into their pen—

having come, we guessed, through the grade school lunchroom
garbage that Dad collected in too-heavy
barrels every day, the swill he fed them on

because grain was expensive and money was for rent,
electricity, and propane, not for hog feed,
not for anything we could get some other way;

and it was easy to see that the other way regularly came down
to pain in the end, mere battered knuckles or a sore back
from lugging barrels or drums if we were lucky,

so how could we question it and what were we to do
if instead, against our will and in spite of our struggles,
the web of our ways should lead us to the fire?

Storytellers
Grandpa tells one and I whisper back

Wellsir, this bear was the biggest ever seen
    Always say "wellsir," always have a bear.
a head like a rockin chair, a sneer on its jaw,
    Make it as big as something on the farm
its two front paws like the hoods of cars.
    like a tree, a truck, or a stack of baled hay.
It stood up like a man to snuffle the breeze,
    Make everyone think it'll do somethin bad
then smashed through the brush toward me at a gallop
    but then let it do what no one expected:

    Wellsir, this bear was the size of a windmill
I threw my gun down and got up a sycamore,
    and it had its arms going like a windmill too.
but he chewed on that tree with his big nasty teeth
    It throwed me straight up about as high as a barn
till he chopped it plumb down and I fell down with it.
    and opened his mouth so it looked like a stock tank
Reckon what happened? That big bear swallered me!
    and down I went into his old fat belly.
That's how we all got here inside this bear!
    I could see out bear eyes and hear with bear ears,
It's daytime when he's awake and the rest of the time dark,
    because a story ends however you say it does.
and nobody knows where that old bear is headed.

Skinning

Grandpa's knife could slit a dead squirrel's skin
across its backbone, never mark the meat,
and hardly leave a drop of blood behind.

I'd sit astride the bench and the hind feet
would fall to me. He'd straddle at the head.
We'd dig our fingernails into the cut

and pull both ways until we peeled the hide
from the flesh, inside out like two thick socks.
It set my teeth, the tearing sound it made.

He'd have two wash pans waiting on a rock:
one was for the heads and guts, the mess
our mess of squirrels left, slop for the hogs—

the other one was for the meat he'd dress,
the knife point picking off the hairs that strayed
onto our supper, onto that glistening flesh

that made me stare, that made me feel so strange,
because—I didn't quite know, couldn't spin
it out. I'd never seen inside of things

before, the body opened like a bin
or sack, the nakedness beneath the skin.

Picking Poke

No one had to tell me: we never spent on *anything*
if a substitute could be had for free,

so I followed my mother to trek the snaking
tree line of Adams Creek, looking

for the purpley stalks of poke, the weed
we gathered every summer to eat,

its feather-shaped leaves boiled and rinsed
three times so it looked like the spinach

we hadn't bought. And in our not buying, I became
the intimate of puddled lanes

that cut through creekside tangle, the exchanges
of shikepoke, redbird, raincrow,

little networks of wiggletail and tumblebug,
dogwood, poison ivy, redbud,

the way to wade a slickery cold creek
barefoot with a paper sack

of poke held carefully out of the water, the way
to negotiate agreement with a landscape,

to wander in comfort despite the copperheads and scorpions
we spotted as we searched for our supper greens—

to disappear into washes and dales
and inhabit them, figure in their folds,

until all places wild and unfenced I could consider
mine and myself their diminutive, their familiar.

Letters

He kept it under the divan where it couldn't
get stepped on, chalk and eraser
on top of it: little blackboard

framed in pale pine, slate
on which I fashioned my first crude
letters, his huge hand closing

over mine to help me form them,
to learn the order of things—"A" first,
the upstroke, the downstroke, the cross again

and again until I could generate
a rough lopsided capital on my own
and on through "Z," through zero

through nine—months passing as we framed
daily the strange awkward marks
whose insistent, eccentric gravity

I could feel but not account for, impossible
fascination of what chalk created,
eraser destroyed, both

by erosion, both in the single
clasp of that double hand
in that little clutch of moments left to him

before a final stroke closed in and left me
without him, with only these odd characters,
these letters, this way.

God Was Underground

I didn't catch on when they first put Grandpa
in that big blue box in the fancy room.

Everyone was real still except when they cried,
and they all kept looking at their feet.

They said Grandpa was going to meet God that day,
and that was why he was dressed up in a suit.

I thought God would have heavy sad eyes
and long blond hair like a girl's,

and him and Grandpa would smile and shake hands,
but that was before I saw what happens.

They put his metal box in a big deep hole
in a kind of park, and we had to throw dirt on it.

So it must have been that God was already down there,
and God was dead too, the same as Grandpa.

I didn't think dead people could talk to each other
underground without moving their mouths.

So maybe God was like the little red worms
Grandpa and me would dig to fish with—

maybe He stayed underground with no eyes
and no face and made you feel squirmy.

Maybe when you go to meet God, it's a lot
like going down in the ground to meet the worms,

you and God both just quiet in the dirt,
and you stay a long time and look at your feet.

Bear Stories

When the bare bulbs on wires in the high ceilings flickered
and sooty water dripped from the flue hole

and lightning broke so hard you saw a part of God
through the jagged cracks that lit the clouds

green and black like a bruise, we all would go down
in Aunt Lucy's storm cellar among her jars of beet pickles

and strawberry jam until the tornadoes had passed, a circle
of kitchen chairs in the half-light of a coal oil lamp—

Uncle Short telling the one about the twister that turned
an old boy's house into toothpicks and left him

in the bathtub without a scratch on him, and Aunt Gertie
how a storm had left a house alone but tore

the cellar out of the ground and killed everyone in it—
and in spite of my being five, they'd ask if I'd killed

any bears lately, and I'd allow how I'd shot at one
and missed and that bear'd got so mad he'd busted

my gun all to pieces over a stump, and I'd finally
had to jump off a cliff into the water to get shut

of that dang bear, and everybody'd laugh,
and some cousin would say, "It's about stopped,"

and we'd peek out the door at the leaves and twigs
scattered down the drive, Aunt Lucy saying, "Well,

the old house is still standin," and we'd go home,
the lightning just some flickers now far off to the east.

Colored

Most grown-ups I knew used a different word,
a bad word they told me not to take up,

but Grandma always said *colored*
in a kind of high whisper—*There's a colored*

man at the door—like his skin was some secret
we had all agreed he shouldn't be told of,

something we ought to keep from him or maybe,
like a patch on someone's clothes, a thing to be

silent about even though everyone knew.
We all knew, too, who the man was—the only

black man who ever came around to our place,
the only black man I had ever heard speak—

and we all went outside to the battered box
truck to look at the produce he'd brought

to sell, and the grown-ups haggled over sweet
potatoes and cantaloupes or traded eggs

and milk for roastin ears and green cabbages,
thanked the man politely, and told him to stop

again next time. But it was plain as air:
they used words gingerly when he was with us,

and I could feel a strange presence hanging there
in the space between them, a low unseen fence

or invisible rail they wouldn't straddle
made of something so heavy it couldn't be lifted.

Octobers

Dad would lug the big coal stove in
off the porch where it had rusted all summer and fit
the pipe to the hole in the chimney—covered
until now with a pie pan—and bring in the coal box;
and with the front room smaller, I could see ahead
how that one warm room would draw us all to it,

always somebody stabbing at the fire
with the crowbar we used for a poker, someone
working the grate back and forth, adding to the din
getting rid of the clinkers or tumbling fresh coal
into the flames, banging down the iron lid, always
everyone talking in that one warm place

with the TV going and nobody watching it,
somebody singing with a guitar, one of the aunts
telling a big story to the others leaning in
(*and I want you to know* . . . she'd say and *I'll be
jiggered if he didn't* . . .), while Grandma cracked
pecans with a tack hammer and the cousins argued—

whose hound, whose car—my younger sister
riding her trike in slow circles across the linoleum,
uncles laughing at her, smoking pipes or rolling
their own, opening the stove with one
smooth motion to toss a spent match or butt
so quick its warm breath was all I noticed.

COUNTRY BOY

Sounding It Out

teacher and student

We're going to learn to read with a book called
Tip
is my dog's name too Tippy really but he's black not
a brown dog with white-tipped tail
boys and girls now sound out the words with me
Will-Tip-Be-Good?
you know he will nobody ever gets dirty old Tip doesn't
get dirty even when he's digging up the flowerbeds in
the pictures in this book
are like special words to help you read the
other words
it's all perfectly clean even the mittens Tip drags around
this nice house
has a nice boy and girl what are their names everyone
sound it out now JUH AH KUH
Jack-and-Ja-net
wear good clothes and shoes to play in and nobody
argues about money when they buy
A Bed and a Dish for Tip
is the name of this chapter children and tomorrow the kitten
will get to share the bed and dish because
everyone can get along
better in books than they can at home because
there's Tip you know and then there's Tippy

Milking Time

I sat sideways on the ledge of a weathered barn
window in a long file of barn windows,
my feet above our milk-cow's head, listening
to the tinny sounds of the first streams of milk
to hit the galvanized bucket changing slowly
to a deeper sound, more hollow, a clock
almost that told me how long before dark,
the light fading already inside the walls
where my mother worked below on her milking stool,
the west-facing slope still bright on my other side,
the landlord's Holsteins standing perfectly still
on their cow paths in the grass, none of them chewing,
and even the wind, so rarely absent there,
no longer moving the clumps of weeds.

I knew the well was going dry again
and we'd have to haul water, that our car
wasn't running and Dad couldn't figure why,
that we didn't have any money and wouldn't.
But it all fell away into that motionless hillside
as it grew paler and the shadow of the barn
grew softer, the moments unfolding only
with the sound of milk on milk
and the hazy light that fell from that place
so slowly I could barely tell it was going.

Country Boy

Why did I cringe at the unvarnished shock
in the voice of the first boy to look down from the bus
at my family's falling-down wreck of a farm
off the dirt road behind his nice subdivision?

He stared at me, unbelieving: "You *LIVE* there?"
How had I missed it before then, the heft
such speech could bear?
                                And how did I answer
in the hearing of his friends and still feel surprise

the following morning when all of them were waiting
with their new club of words? *Cracker boy. Cornbread.*
Tax stealer. And how, of all catcalls, did the mildest
and truest enrage me the most: *country boy?*

Country boy: their leader chanted it, dropping
his tongue to the floor of his mouth to mock
my accent and make it obscene, *cuntra boa,*
cuntra boa, until I learned that words could make *me*

obscene, till I calculated daily whether I had the strength,
if I caught him off guard, to slam his face
into the metal bar on the back of the bus seat,
to pay him for those weights, that name that was my fall.

Mirrow

When I said, *Look in nat little winder,*
I meant only to show a classmate
the new chicks cheeping in the incubator
in the back of our room and to celebrate
their hatching. But my pretty teacher,
the smiling, shining object of my first great
unreflective crush, saw a lesson: *It's window,*
not winder. And pillow, not piller. Bellow,

fellow, and wallow. She went on in a strange whisper:
A teacher teaches. A fighter fights.
But yeller doesn't yell—do you see? So yeller
is yellow, yellow! Will you repeat
yellow with me?
                 I said *yellow*, longing to cover
my face and bury it, to swear to hate
my treacherous mouth forever.
                         Shallow
habits of speech reflect a shallow

character, she said then, hand on my shoulder,
and I wasn't sure whether to nod or shake,
so I retreated to my desk.
                    That night, my mother
quizzed me about coming home with an unhappy face:
Come and look at yourself in the mirror.
                       Mirror!
I burst out. *Mirror? The teacher explained*
all of that today. It doesn't mirr. No.
So it's not a mirror, not a mirror. It's a mirrow.

Return

Suddenly I craved recess from that noisy
house, from that pack, from much older cousins
and all those aunts and uncles, half a dozen
at a time who laughed at my teasing stories.
Their voices seemed to multiply and push me
outside somehow. I didn't know the reason
exactly: it was not some new aversion
to them—I loved *them*—but to any company
at all. And so I learned to disappear
into the space beneath the ball-like bush
out front, to part its thick soft leaves and sheer
white flowers and rest in its green womb, to push
my spine against its barky spine, to peer
at my dog Elvis smiling in that hushed
cool world until a fresh
strange little tune made itself in my mind
and spilled out whispered on my lips, a kind
of story bound to steer
itself by song, a story I would tell
them all when I went back, whenever I fell
to wanting them, the spell
of silence undone by a little wash
of loneliness I knew would push me, force
me back to that packed house.

Commodities

I loved how our old green-and-white high-finned '59
Chrysler, cruising down the highway, made a shadow
like the Batmobile that glided over ditches and train tracks,
easily and immediately transforming itself always
into the shape of what it encountered, bulging
with a telegraph pole, dipping over a mudhole, following us
all the way to town.
                   But Dad acted funny
when we got to the courthouse. In a line that said COMMODITIES,
he stood stiff and didn't talk. So I asked, "What's comma-ditties?"
and he said, "It's like groceries." Then, when I didn't say anything,
"Be quiet now."
                  So I looked around at the ragged
men and women in line with us, their sun-cracked faces,
none of them talking or joking like grownups
at home, three black kids I knew I wasn't allowed
to play with beside their mother on a bench across the floor,
everyone rigid and silent.
                 The man at the window
put a pasteboard box on the counter when we got there,
and I could see he put in a big plastic sack
of beans and a cloth bag that said CORNMEAL. Dad
hesitated when the box was pushed toward us.
                       "I work hard,
ever day," he said, and the man nodded. We walked
out the double doors with that box, down long steps with our food,
back to the old beat-up Chrysler, back home in silence,
me watching the shadow still changing beside us.

All Day

All day records falling on the turntable, all day
Mom at the ironing board pressing clothes
the wives of insurance men and evangelists brought
at fifty cents a bushel basket, their sheets,
tablecloths, dresses, their husband's slacks.
All day the house full of country music,
she played Hank, she put on Patsy
and the other Hank, she played the click of iron,
its hiss on the film of spray starch.
She put on Ernest and Johnny and the funny
stink of hot metal on the underarm of a banker's
dress shirt, on the button of a Tulsa oil man.
She was Walkin after Midnight, broke and lonely,
she was waiting for Sunday Morning. She sang along
with Kitty and Buck, playing the cascade
of ice down a mason jar of sugar-charged tea,
working on the handkerchiefs and neckties of real estate
agents. She was George on White Lightnin,
she was Movin On, she was Marty
in El Paso. All day playing
the metal hangers she lined up
on a long piece of baling wire stretched
tight across the corner between two nails.

Elvis

Words don't make sense, *I said to Elvis,*
stroking his head. Elvis was my dog.
Just listen to this: Elvis. Elvis.
You're Elvis, aren't you? Elvis.
You hear that? Elvis Elvis Elvis
Selva Selva-sel Vasell Vasell Vasell-vis.
He looked at me with a big smile on his face
and a tongue hanging way down dripping.
It works on clothesline, chickenhouse,
windmill, all words. All you have to do
is keep on saying it and a word goes
all funny and the thing it means goes away.
It's still there, I mean, but it's like when you twirl
around and around with your arms out,
and something is still over there going by the tips
of your fingers—stock tank, hay barn, privy—
all still there, but now they're a blur you can't catch
up with, and when you try to look at them, they keep
on going, and then you laugh and fall down,
and you get dizzy again on the ground
before they come back and their words come back
to where they were before you started saying Elvis
Elvis—Elvis! You're not Elvis, are you, boy?

Storyin

Don't story to me, Grandma would say.
She meant "lie"—*Don't lie*
to me—but she couldn't bring herself to say
that word she found so vile,
as if what mattered was the ring of language and not the thing
it described, the sound and not the truth, though truth was
  obviously why
she had spoken to begin with.
                              So when I flung
a hairspray can into the trash fire she was tending, it was, in a way,

because the label said
DO NOT PUNCTURE OR INCINERATE CAN
all in capitals in bright red
print, and I couldn't stand
not knowing why it used that word "incinerate," why it implied
a story it wouldn't tell the ending of. When it exploded, the can
flew across the pasture, spreading fire
over the tall grass, red breaking through tangles of dead

weeds, the whole field ablaze
by the time we got help, men
soaking gunny sacks in the stock tank and beating out the flames,
defending the barn and the hen-
house and the farmhouse they somehow rescued from harm.
And when it was out, Grandma rushing to tell everyone
there on the blackened and smoking farm
the story of how she let the fire get away, how she was the one
  to blame.

Lookin Beans

The kitchen table is buried in pintos.
Mom and Grandma pick out the bad ones,
the rocks, the sticks, the pieces of hull,
and rake the good ones over the edge
and let them drop into pans on their laps:

I know how to do this. *You better go slower*
I've looked beans before! *or the rocks and the sticks*
Do you think I can't feel *will be in our dinner.*
the barbs you throw out *Now don't get all huffy*
to stick me with? *and go off and sulk.*

You're like an old porcupine, *I'll tell you what you are:*
one everyone knows *you're the Cimarron River.*
has been eatin dynamite. *A woman like you*
It rattles its quills out, *one time put some beans on,*
sticks spines in the livestock, *and they simmered and simmered,*
and devours all the tender *but they never got tender,*
plants in the garden, *so that woman got mad*
but no one will dream *just the way you do,*
of throwin rocks at it *and she up and threw that pot*
or takin a pot shot. *of beans in the river.*

They're afraid it'll go off *Even in the water*
and blow the whole farm *those beans kept on cookin.*
from here to the river. *To this day they're still cookin.*
So it stays on, stickin em. *Just Cimarron and Cimarron.*

Icebreaking

In my father's right hand, the shaft
of an axe left too long to the rain:
crooked in his left elbow, the double blade.

On his sleeve, the dull signature of rust.

*

Some mornings the ice is like asphalt,
the first blow a bright gash in its surface.
Other mornings it is just brittle and dark.

He exhales a long plume of steam.

*

If you don't open up enough water,
they'll crowd each other onto the ice:
one of them will fall through, guaranteed.

He sidles down the pond's glazed edge.

*

The axe dissolves in the bitter air
over his head, reappears darker and colder
in the black mouth where cattle drink.

Fissures lace his feet like spider webs.

*

He slams the battered tailgate. Only then,
from brown, ratty weeds in the frozen mud
do sparrows rise, small and drab,

each like the shadow of a single hand.

AN

OCCURRENCE

ON THE

BLUEBIRD

Starling

Big boys pecked at me on the schoolbus,
arms folded on the seatbacks in front of me
and behind—the biggest one perched high

across the aisle cawing *trailer trash! ha!*
free lunch! ha! welfare rat! and any peep
of explanation (*we pay for my lunch ticket,*

we're not on welfare, we don't have a trailer)
only set them all bobbing and shrieking.
At home with my BB gun, I wandered

the pastures, just walking, the gunstock
under my arm. There was something comforting
in carrying that little rifle, as though it could

give me some say.
                        Starlings were lined up
on the barn roof, and without knowing why,
I lifted the gun to my shoulder. Only one

lone bird failed to fly. I sighted it
down the barrel, and I made myself despise it
for being so tame, so unguarded, so available

to be shot at. The ball hit its shoulder,
and it skittered off the roof, alive but with a ruined
wing. I watched ashamed as it fluttered

around the barnyard awhile and then sat still,
waiting now for the blacksnake or passing hawk,
one eye fixed on me, dark and uncomprehending.

First B

Dad and Mom heard simultaneously

Look at that paper, Buddy,   Son, this arithmetic,
them takeaways and plusses.   it's your only paper so far
This is the first B   not a perfect score.
you've ever brought home.   You need to see something:
B's ain't good enough,   you're smarter than we are.
not for you, Buddy.   Your job is to show us
You can do better: what we all coulda been
you can do what I shoulda.   if we'd a-knowed what to do.

See, I made A's too   They got a great tall school
exactly like you,   that they call a college.
but I quit at fifteen   You can go there when you get big.
to work, to make money.   It costs a lot of money,
Don't do what I done.   and none of us have been,
You can show me up, Buddy,   but we hear they let you
have a job not so hard,   go up there for free
not hay somebody's cattle,   if they see how smart you are,
haul slop for old hogs,   if you make all A's.
fix fence, and work on   No one we know
old cars every night   has gotten that far,
for a few extra dollars.   so you'll have to show us.

You'll have to know them books,   We want you to go, son,
them takeaways and plusses.   though it's a long ways off.
You got to get it right   You're the one who can,
all the time, Buddy.   so you're the one who has to.

Mrs. Greenley

Even though she was wrinkly and held the corner
of her mouth in a fixed, down-turned knot—

and though she went buggy about the use of dull pencils,
the way we handled scissors, our rate of consumption
of red construction paper and white paste—

and although she got spooked if you chewed on a crayon
and made you wash your mouth out with Listerine
and rinse it out three times with cold water afterwards—

and even if she poured red sawdust floor sweep
everywhere in her tile-floored, second-grade domain
and herded it constantly into piles with a push broom,
enlisting us all to scoop it up in dustpans
with her scratchy "Let's keep it clean, boys and girls!"—

for all that, I still loved her, because everyone knew
she read the best stories of any teacher in the school.
Every day she made us clean up following lunch,
and then we sat in our seats with our foreheads down
on the cool tops of our desks, every eye closed,
each of us imagining for the next twenty minutes
what it felt like to be someone else: a family
who went to Kansas in a covered wagon, a boy
who killed giants for the king, a stuffed rabbit, a pig,
a girl who had a dream about a deck of cards,
a man who accidentally learned a magic word.

Visitation of the Well-Fed Preacher
a kind of invitation to his church

I made a show of drawing in the dirt with a stick
so I could stay while the preacher spoke to my father
in the tottery little barn he used for a garage:

God doesn't want you, brother, he said,
slathered and slimed with the grease from axles
and the oil that drains from the bowels of crankcases
or, like the Prodigal, mired in feeding swine.
No, God has a beautiful plan for your life!

Dad just grinned and kept turning the wrench.
I drew a tubby pig with wheels on its feet.

Why then do you choose—he gestured toward our house now—
to live in a hovel, unpainted and blackened
with coal smoke streaming from a filthy chimney
on a bedraggled farm with a stinking privy
and barns and sheds on the brink of collapse?

Beats settin out in the weather, Reverend.
I doodled a fat outhouse with a stovepipe hat.

For God didn't make you, he went on without stopping,
to drive some old wreck you cobbled together
out of parts from the hulks that line your drive,
for your kids to appear in public in hand-me-downs,
or for beans and potatoes to be your every meal.

He's got a hell of a way of showin it, Preacher.
I scratched out a chubby man with patches on his elbows.

The Price of Three Eggs

At first I could only stare as it gaped
and squirmed to engulf the first
smooth white egg that lay along the dark

wall of the chicken house. It moved slowly,
almost leisurely, toward the next. I yelled
to Dad that a big snake was eating our

breakfast again, but by the time he arrived
with the long-handled hoe, it was sliding
up to the third egg, the others now twin

bulges behind its head. It would have taken
everything, the food we were depending on
that morning, more eggs other mornings,

the spares we could have sold to pay some
little debt. Dad raised the hoe, brought it
down hard, severing the animal's head:

the body writhed and jerked, smashing
the one remaining egg and smearing itself
in yolk and white and blood, dying the way snakes

always died, as if they were bent on coming back,
as if they could always return to make us pay.

The Loft

I climbed up in the moonlit loft
and sat there on the hay:

> *Repeating "na-na-na" to myself in a soft*
> *whisper was my inadequate defense for the facts,*

I wanted just to get away
from every human voice,

> *from her angry wailing desperation, his low inexact*
> *grunts in reply, as though both had lost the skill*

to hide from people making noise.
I wanted to be still

> *to speak or to stop speaking, as though their voices had caught*
> *on some middle snag, some thorn of language they could not free*

and safe from all the harsh and shrill
things they still screamed inside,

> *their mouths from. I stroked a barn cat, sought*
> *relief in its purring, in my "na-na-na's," in the sweet*

but found no matter what I tried
their voices hectored me.

> *hum of a sad song, anything to stop what they*
> *continued in my mind, in that dark and tangled hay.*

Sleepwalking

How far I'd walked and why, I'd never know,
but I could rise and dress and venture out
onto the moonlit farm, to distant fields,
wearing my coat if it were cold, all while
I was asleep.
          Deep in a vivid dream
of another nearby place, I'd wake and feel
that I had been ghosted away, transported:
loafing on the porch while Dad played guitar
or watching while Mom laid the supper table,
I'd suddenly find myself among the boulders
beside the dark creek, puzzled as to what
I could be doing there, far from my bed
while heat lightning flashed against the midnight sky.
In a mere instant I could go from walking
a certain cow path in full noontime sun
to stumbling off that same path in the pitch
dark, dead broom grass crunching underfoot.
It was as if I'd merged with those broad pastures
and ponds and scrubby copses so completely
that even parts I never looked upon
became as much a part of me as those
I saw by day.
          All unaware of dangers
and dumb to pleasures I was passing by,
I found myself in places I was dreaming.

Episode of the Encyclopedia Salesman

I knew better than to ask for things we couldn't afford
and even at seven had taught myself not to want them—but I wanted
those books with the red rectangles on their spines, Colliers'
huge black volumes that the stranger extracted
from his black case and lined up on our linoleum.
                                              I knew Grandma
thought he had a gun in there, what she always thought
about strangers like this one in shiny black shoes and white
shirt and dark tie, who sat on the flowered yellow
kitchen chair next to our coal stove.
                                              And I knew Dad
would say *no, we can't pay for them*, that Mom would say *no,
they're free at the library*, that my smart aleck cousin
would ask *Why don't you show us some big heavy books?*

I was wrong, though: Dad looked straight at me.
*There's an old car I could overhaul that would bring the money
if you think you could use these.*
                                              The room got quiet.
I waited for Uncle Fred to say something like *Hell,
if he reads all them, he'll be purt near smart as me.*
But the silence held, a first in that house,
so I just mumbled *Yessir, I spect I could,*

as though I had no idea, even at seven,
of what my *yessir* meant to everyone present:
another month of beans, less coal for the fire,
my father's spending his winter evenings with a drop light
in the unheated barn he used for a garage—
the real price of privilege, its great black bulk.

Old Snowball

I wasn't supposed to get out of Old Snowball,
our battered white pickup. But Dad had seen
a friend and gone to jaw, so when the first
few shovelfuls of coal had clattered down
in Snowball's bed behind me, I climbed out.

A black man had the shovel: he was old,
bent down as though the coal had warped his back
somehow. His overalls and shirt were dark,
his thick work gloves filthy, coated with grime.

I knew that I was not allowed to talk
to him, so I just stood and watched him work.
He jabbed the shovel into the glittering pile,
levering coal into the truck: dust flew
around us for a bit, and then he dropped
the shovel on the pile, pulled off his gloves,
and rested his hands on the tailgate top.
They were not black, those hands. I thought they looked
like chocolate milk, and not at all like coal.

I knew that I would probably get in trouble
for getting dirty, but I made a mark
in the grime on that truck, a line that showed
the white of Old Snowball, the black shards in its bed,
the man's hands in between, my hands like chips
or bread, the little dust spots settling over it all.

Story Time Girl

City-County Public Library

Of course I loved her miniskirt and bob-
cut and the tinge of effervescent green
that flashed each time she blinked—how could I *not*
when she was so grown up, but with a sheen
coming from every part of her? No girl
I'd ever seen had dressed like her, had hair
or eyes like her, or seemed—like her—from a world
so distant from mine. I knew not to stare,
but I did it anyway.
                         Yet what I saw
was nothing to compare with what I heard:
she told the red death and the yellow wall-
paper and the great jumping frog, each word
sharp and dangerous, each one with a glint
as sure and momentary as the hint

of shimmer on her lids. I couldn't take
my ears off her: she was like a library
within the library—the place I prized
most, where every adult I knew advised
me that my future lay. A solitary
book, all of them said, would be the book
that left my way distinct and undisguised
and cleared a path for me and swept it clean.
I felt it coming toward me from those green-
                         hazed eyes.

An Occurrence on the Bluebird

We called our mustard-colored school bus *the Bluebird*
because that's what the chrome plate by the door said,
and none of us would challenge that word.

> I sat by

Lionel, the other boy on the bus who liked
to read, the one who seemed unaffected by name-
calling, the one who stopped the others' taunting me

because my family was poor.

> One day the Bluebird crested

the low ridge above the desperate little farm
where I lived, and Lionel looked up from his book:

> *Are you guys hillbillies?*

His voice was soft and serious, and I knew he was trying
to find a place to put me, to think of a name
that would fit me somehow. And I knew

that a name was a verdict and a kind of sentence,
that even for Lionel, *hillbilly* would make my high-hoping
and sober father into a drunk, bearded and quick

to his gun, and my pretty mother into a toothless
horror, all of us into things vicious, lazy,
and filthy, and would fix us that way forever

in his mind. So I said, *No. We just don't have much money.*
Then I pulled up my sleeves and held out my bare arms. *Look,*
though, look! I'm every bit as clean as you, not dirty at all.

THE TIME

I DIDN'T

DROWN

Third Grade, Two Licks, First Day

Raising my hand, did I lift my middle finger,
not understanding that it was obscene?
Or was she angling to produce a quiver
in any first-day third-grader still green
enough to dare to question anything
in that classroom? Or had she simply caught
the heavy twang in my voice and so spot-

ted me as poor?
     And is it worth the bother
at this late date to excavate the reasons
why one person would want to strike another?
I think we know already that such reasons
exist only as phantoms, the bitter leavings
of our frustration.
     Come along, she called.
I have something for you—it's out in the hall.

I went. She pointed out a little line
of shiny pennies, three on the tile floor,
and told me *Take those home.*
     But they're not mine.
Go on. I'm giving them to you. They're yours.
I bent over: *They're all glued to the floor.*
I never saw the paddle, but she hit
me with it on the word "floor," two times quick.

I forced a laugh, but my face went all hot
when she commanded me back to my seat,
surprised, ashamed, but unaware of what.

The Day of the Swarm

the bees swirled down all around me in long buzzing ropes

from under one of the many warped siding pieces

on our house that were forever loosening, slipping,
struggling against the persevering facts of weather

and gravity, against the tendency of this life
to lower, bees everywhere spiraling to a point
on the trunk of the sapling I had been playing by

where a ball of bees my size now hung as if waiting
for the bee man who had come to take them to a new
home. *Don't fidget,* he told me. *You just have to be brave,
and let them crawl all over you, because if you're still
and don't touch or swat them, they'll like you and not sting you,*

and I told him I would stay brave, and somehow he caught
the queen and put her in the big white box he had brought
and set beneath the tree. He tapped the trunk and all
that great wad of bees fell straight down together like one
creature into the box, and when they had settled down,
he put the lid on, and I felt the ones on my arms
and the back of my neck begin to whirr and leave me
for the hole in the end of their new house, their new white

perfect house the beekeeper would soon load in his truck.
And something was there, hovering behind the bee man,
behind the sapling, the bees mumbling inside their hive.
The measure of a life, no matter the circumstance.
Its constant, incremental decay. Its sweet despite.

Layin on Quilts Lookin Up at the Night

voices out of the dark

My old granny would say
a giant dog flew up there,
spilled across the sky
a road of white cornmeal.
And seven boys climbed up
whose mothers didn't feed them.
Didn't Granddad show us stars once
he called Lou's Chain?
I don't know who Lou was.
Another set he claimed
was the path the dead walk
when they're movin on
to wherever they go.
Nobody knows, of course,
exactly where that is,
but they meet God someways.
I just wonder how it would be
if you could get up there and live,
in the stars I mean,
on another world someplace.
How would you walk there
or eat or get money?
And would people be different,
and would you get along easier?

That box of stars
makes the bowl of the Dipper
and the other three the handle.
Some of the old-timers
could show you seven sisters
or a hen and her chicks
you could tell the time of night by.
They still hold in my mind,
but I don't know where to look.
They're just big bonfires
hangin in the sky,
but they're so far away,
they start to look tiny,
like little pin holes
in a piece of black cloth.
It's like when you're layin
with your head upside down
off the side of the bed
till the ceiling looks like a floor
with light bulbs stickin up,
with humps to climb over
to get out the door,
with really low windows
all openin from the top.

Walker of Fields

I sought out on cow paths alone the lone
oak among acres of pasture where Elvis
my shepherd was buried the rope end
tire I emptied after storms the water the rusted
windmill pumped to the bucket for drinking for bathing
the stock tank the clothesline our silhouettes
fluttered on warm days stiffened on cold
coal pile my red Western Flyer wagon hauled
bit by bit to the box on the porch gray scrap wood
pile bumblebees stung my sisters on whether laughing
or crying at the time unsure hay barn we milked
Old Babe's weedy-tasting milk in Tippy killed
the big snake in and shook and shook
it heap of old tires a little ghost
scorpion found my hand on ponds I fished for sun-
fish among uncles path from the front taken
only by evangelists and salesmen path we all took
in back to the privy the chicken house snakes
hunted eggs in skunks and raccoons
searched for openings to little cavity in a rocky
rise in a far pasture one of the cousins
claimed to scare me was the hole the booger
man came out of but I saw little red
foxes go into enough that I knew

Don't Three Halves Make One-and-a-Half, Ma'am?

a kind of argument in third-grade math

Say your mom baked three pies for Thanksgiving,
    Three pies? We never have that many, ma'am,
and your family ate half the pecan, half the rhubarb,
    and my grandma and my aunts make the pies at our house,
and half the pumpkin. Now, what would you have left?
    and with all my cousins there wouldn't be any left.
Three halves. Do you see?
                    Yes, ma'am, so you're saying
    it's three halves of anything, half a roll of rusted wire,
Now tell me, do you really not understand this,
    half the tin roof that was blown off our chicken house,
or don't you just want to argue and waste
    and the other half of the fence post we chopped up for kindling,
half of our class time, half of our math time?
    but it's still three halves?
                  No, that's not three halves!
It's not three halves unless they're all the same,
    Three pies aren't the same. Rhubarb? Yuck!
unless they're all equal, because they're all pies,
    But the things I named are all equal,
equal like leftover half pies at Thanksgiving,
    three halves of pieces of junk in our barnyard,
the same shape and size. Don't you understand equal?
    so I guess I don't see what equals equals,
Or do you just need to visit the principal?
    guess I don't see how to count, ma'am. No, I don't.

Mr. Moore

The coin-op laundry was like a narrow cave
he scuffed around in, wheeling a mop bucket,
moving with a pronounced limp, yelling at me
when Mom focused on the washing and I took
the opportunity to push the basket-
on-wheels down the aisle or climb penniless
onto the penny scale that read out people's
weight and revealed their fortunes on printed cards
that littered the sill of the picture window
in front. I learned a way to fold them to make
little boats and launched them down the concrete trough
of drain water that ran between back-to-back
rows of washers. I'd watch my miniature crafts
thread their way through the tangles of black water-
hose, swirl with soap suds in the eddies of machine
outflows, and trace death spirals around the drain
at the other end, where I'd collect them
on the sly and put them in the big trash bin
before I made more: Mr. Moore got cranky
if the pipe clogged, and he didn't take to boats
much in the first place. He was short and gnarled,
and he never smiled. He could have been scary,
but that big limp made him so conspicuous,
he never surprised me or found my ships in time.

Kind of Indians

When my sister was five, she stuck
a crow feather in her dark blonde
hair and danced across our yard,
and when I asked, she said, *We're Indians.*

Mom said. I knew where she'd learned
the dance: Mom took us to powwows
where boys in buckskin and brilliant
feathers, scarlet and turquoise in great

wheels over their heads and backs, and silver
jingles on their ankles moved like gods
to the hypnotic pum-pum of the drum. *Are you sure?*
She stuck out her tongue. *Mom's granny*

was an Indian, so we're Indians. I knew
Mom really had said that part about her granny,
and we went to powwow a lot, so maybe
we were kind of Indians even if our skin and hair

didn't match with those boys in their wonderful feathers.
And if we were kind of Indians without looking
like Indians, couldn't we be anything?—
because we didn't even know all our grannies,

and maybe our grannies didn't know all theirs.
So could we be kind of black and not
know it too? Or kind of Chinese? Kind of
someone we would never even meet?

Trio

everyone talks at once

We got a note from the school that you won't wash your hands
  You don't give any trouble about washing at home.
    See they got this hand washing fountain in the cafeteria

before you eat lunch. You're liable to smell
  You even take baths without any fuss:
    but the water is all stinky like the city pool—

or even get sick if you don't keep clean.
  you help carry the well-water to boil on the stove
    you know that funny smell city water has?—

You always watch when I wash up after work,
  and the soft water from the rain barrel to rinse your hair,
    their water makes you smell like the school nurse's medicine

when I use the Boraxo and the Lava Soap.
  and you stay in that metal tub on the kitchen floor
    that she makes you take if you say you don't wear shoes

You stand by the wash stand and stare into the wash pan
  until the water goes frigid—I leave the kitchen burners on
    at home in the summer. That nurse thinks I'm dirty

while I take all the black and the grease off my hands
  for fear you'll take cold before I make you get out,
    when I'm really clean, so I don't wash at school

and dry off to come to the table for supper.
  so I don't see why you won't scrub before lunch.
    because how can you get clean in dirty water?

No Other Meal

No call to turn it into a soap opera,
but Thanksgiving got close that year somehow
without our knowing what dinner would be.
We wouldn't have gone hungry: we had pinto
beans, surplus that the government doled out,
and lots of taters from that summer's garden,
and though it would have meant losing its eggs
for good, we probably could have simply killed
a chicken, Grandma standing on its feet,
putting the tines of an old garden rake
over its head, and giving one sharp pull.

But no. A strange wild honking came to us
at dawn, waking the darkened house, and Dad
took the shotgun and crawled across the pasture
to shoot the late-flying goose that had landed
so inexplicably among dead broom
grass and cow chips. And so it was no chicken
that Mom scalded and singed the feathers from,
and opened up from the bottom, and dressed
the giblets out and fed the hogs the guts of,
and Grandma stuffed with stale cornbread and sage.

And all the cousins, when they finished eating,
said how damn lucky we had gotten, said
there never was no other meal, not ever.

The Headless Man

reading while listening to Uncle Fred and Grandma argue

"If I can but reach that bridge,"
thought Ichabod, "I am safe."
Just then he heard the black steed
panting and blowing; he fancied
even that he felt his hot breath.
Now Ichabod cast a look
to see if his pursuer
should vanish in a flash of
fire and brimstone. He saw
the goblin rising in his
stirrups and in the very
act of hurling his head
at him. Ichabod endeavored
to dodge the horrible missile,
but too late. It encountered
his cranium with a
tremendous crash—he tumbled
headlong in the dust and
the black steed and the goblin
rider passed like a whirlwind

They say be sure not to cross
Old Adams Bridge at midnight:
that's when the Headless Man jumps
in the back seat of your car
and rides with you for a mile
luggin his old head and then
he just up and disappears.
The poor old feller helped build
that bridge and a cable snapped,
and the end of it tore his
head clean off, and now he tries
to get a lift, to hitch his way
to get his head put back on—
If that boy wasn't settin there,
his nose pasted in that book,
flippin through pages like a
dirt devil flips through dead leaves,
you'd have him scared plumb silly.
Don't you have no better head
your own self than to tell such stuff?

The Time I Didn't Drown

In the middle of ice, I heard the sharp crack
and saw the long fissure streak its silver beneath me,
and I hung there over the farm pond and held my breath.

Would my family find me locked in place that evening,
my blue hood frozen in the pose it had struck
when I stopped struggling? And would it fracture something

in them that I was dead, the boy they all expected
to break out of the life they lived in that place,
the one who might have shown it was *possible* to leave,

even for the ones who stayed?
                              I slid forward gingerly,
not lifting my feet, and slipped off that mirrored surface,
and took a path dark with frozen mud and manure,

rutted with the hoof prints of the landlord's Holsteins,
and walked it past the barn in the blue winter twilight:
past Old Babe, our Guernsey cow, waiting

at the gate to be milked, impatient as always,
past where the chimney boiled black on the house top
from the front room coal stove that kept us warm,

Dad and some cousins probably talking over the TV,
punctuating their arguments by poking at the fire,
Mom and Grandma silent, starting cornbread and potatoes

in the kitchen, while a big pot of beans simmered on—
our supper, as always.
                        But I hadn't fallen through.
So far I hadn't slipped or fallen through.

ACKNOWLEDGMENTS

Grateful acknowledgment is extended to the following publications and websites, where early versions of some of these poems appeared:

Alabama Literary Review: "Country Boy," "The Day of the Swarm," "Letters," "Octobers," "Old Snowball," "Sleepwalking," "Story Time Girl," "The Time I Didn't Drown"
California Quarterly: "Third Grade, Two Licks, First Day"
Helena Independent Record: "Fate," "An Occurrence on the Bluebird"
Hollins Critic: "An Occurrence on the Bluebird"
Iris: "Icebreaking"
National Endowment for the Arts website: "Small Child Walking on Great Aunts and Uncles"
Poet Lore: "Storyin"
River Styx: "Episode of the Encyclopedia Salesman"
Spoon River Poetry Review: "Mirrow," "Picking Poke"
Tar River Poetry: "Fate," "Skinning"

I thank Virginia Reeves for her generous reading and advice during the revision of these poems. Further thanks is due to the Virginia Center for the Creative Arts for residencies that recharged me again and again, to Carroll College for a yearlong sabbatical leave, and to both the LEAW Foundation and the National Endowment for the Arts for their wonderful fellowship support. All provided time and space to allow me to concentrate on this work. Finally, for her daily support and encouragement, my wife Jane Shawn deserves more gratitude and praise than I can voice.

CAVANKERRY'S MISSION

CavanKerry Press is committed to expanding the reach of poetry to a general readership by publishing poets whose works explore the emotional and psychological landscapes of everyday life.

This book's display font, Latin Condensed, is a variant of the Latin typefaces popularly used for setting American newspaper headlines throughout the second half of the nineteenth century.

The text is set in Perpetua, a transitional serif font designed by the English artist Eric Gill. He also assisted in designing the iconic Johnston font, which has been used on signage throughout London's Underground system for over 100 years.